Table of Contents

True Elephant Stories

A Dolch Classic Basic Reading Book

by Edward W. Dolch and Marguerite P. Dolch

illustrated by Kersti Frigell

The Basic Reading Books

The Basic Reading Books are fun reading books that fill the need for easy-to-read stories for the primary grades. The interest appeal of these true stories will encourage independent reading at the early reading levels.

The stories focus on the 95 Common Nouns and the Dolch 220 Basic Sight Vocabulary. Beyond these simple lists, the books use about two or three new words per page.

This series was prepared under the direction and supervision of Edward W. Dolch, Ph.D.

This series was revised under the direction and supervision of Eleanor Dolch LaRoy and the Dolch Family Trust.

SRA/McGraw-Hill

A Division of The **McGraw·Hill** Companies

Original version copyright © 1958 by Edward W. Dolch.
Copyright © 1999 by SRA/McGraw-Hill. All rights reserved.
Except as permitted under the United States Copyright Act, no part of this publication may be reproduced or distributed in any form or by any means, or stored in a database or retrieval system without prior written permission from the publisher.

Printed in the United States of America.

Send all inquires to:
SRA/McGraw-Hill
8787 Orion Place
Columbus, OH 43240-4027

ISBN 0-02-830807-7

4 5 6 7 8 9 0 QST 04 03

The Fun That Hurt

Alice was an elephant that liked to have fun. She thought it was fun to take something from you and put it in a hole in the hay by her feet. Then, she would go on eating her hay as if she had done nothing at all.

Alice played jokes on the other elephants. Sometimes when the elephants were pushing the big circus wagons, Alice would make you think she was pushing the wagon. But if you looked, you would find that her head was not against the wagon, and the elephant that was working with her was doing all the pushing.

Alice thought that the most fun of all was mashing cans flat. When Alice saw a can, down went a big front foot. There was the can, mashed as flat as could be. Then, Alice would lift her trunk and squeal as if to say, "Look. Look, see what I have done!"

Sometimes when Alice was not very happy, the bull-keeper, who is the man who looks after the elephants, would say to her, "Alice, come with me. I know what will make you happy."

The bull-keeper would take Alice to where people had thrown away cans. Alice would mash can after can as flat as could be. She would be happy and squeal. When there were no more cans to mash, the bull-keeper would take Alice back to the circus.

But one day, something happened to Alice.

It was time to eat. Nearly all of the circus people were in a small tent eating. Alice and another elephant were pushing a big circus wagon on the circus lot. That is, the other elephant was pushing the big wagon, because Alice did not have her head against the wagon. She just seemed to be pushing.

Then, Alice saw something. She saw five big cans just beside the little tent. Alice moved very quietly. An elephant is very big, but it can move so quietly that you cannot hear it.

Alice mashed one of the cans. Then, she stuck her trunk into another can. Alice found something very good. It was apple juice.

Alice stuck her trunk into one of the other cans. She found more apple juice. She thought that it was very good. She stuck her trunk way down into the can to get the very last of the juice.

As she was drinking the last of the juice, up went one of Alice's big front feet. Down it went and mashed the can—right around her trunk.

Suddenly Alice squealed and squealed and squealed. You never heard such a noise. Then, Alice started running, squealing and waving her trunk in the air with the can mashed on the end of it.

Alice pushed over a part of the little tent. She pushed over two big circus wagons. People ran everywhere to get away from the big elephant. She got out of the circus lot and started for the country.

The bull-keeper and many of the circus people got on horses and went after Alice. It took them a long time to find her. She was waving her trunk in the air with the can mashed on the end of it. She was making a loud noise because the can hurt her trunk very much. But Alice was very tired because she had run so fast.

The circus people put chains around Alice's four big legs. The bull-keeper took the can off Alice's trunk. Then, the circus people took the chains away.

Alice looked at the can on the ground. She put one of her big feet on it and mashed it again. Then, she picked up the mashed can with her trunk and threw it as fast as she could. And Alice never mashed another can as long as she lived.

Babe

A long time ago in a park in San
Francisco, there lived a big elephant
named Babe. She was kind and gentle.
The children loved her. Every day when
the air was warm, Babe went walking.
She pulled a red-and-yellow circus
wagon around the park. Many happy
children went riding in the wagon.

This is the story of how Babe came to the park in San Francisco: There was a man who knew how much children love to see elephants. He wanted to give an elephant to the park. He asked Frank Buck, a man who went all over the world getting live animals for zoos and circuses, to get him a big elephant for the park in San Francisco.

Babe Starts to the United States

Frank Buck had a friend at the zoo in Yangon, Myanmar. Yangon, Myanmar is also called Rangoon, Burma. He had a lot of elephants. When the man at the zoo found out that Frank Buck wanted a big elephant, he said Frank could have Babe. Now, how were they going to get Babe from Myanmar to the United States?

Frank Buck owned a farm in the city of Singapore. He kept many animals on the farm until he could send them to the United States. Babe would have to go to his farm in Singapore. Babe had to be put on a ship to get to Singapore.

Babe was a good elephant, but she did not like new things. And going on a ship was something very new. The people had to put a great band around

Babe, and then they pulled her up in the air and put her on the ship. Babe did not like it. Babe was afraid. She made a lot of noise.

By the time the ship got to Singapore, Babe was all right. She walked off the ship and was taken to the farm.

At the farm, Babe was trained to pull a big log. When she got to the United States, she would be trained to pull a wagon. Babe was a good elephant and tried to do what Frank wanted her to do.

At last the time came to put Babe on a ship for the United States. Four more elephants were going to the United States, also. They were not as big as Babe. So, the people put the other elephants on the ship before they tried to put Babe on.

When Babe saw her elephant friends lifted up into the air, she thought of the time she had been lifted. She knew that she did not like going up in the air. Right then Babe knew that she was going to keep her four feet on the ground.

When the people tried to get the big band around Babe, she lay down. They could not make her move. The people gave Babe things to eat. They got big logs and pushed her to her feet, but Babe would let no one get near her. She was not going to let anyone put that big band around her. She was not going to let anyone lift her in the air.

Babe was a good elephant, but she was angry. No one was going to make her go up into the air. And remember, Babe was a very big elephant.

Then Frank Buck thought that with his helpers from the farm who knew Babe, he could get the big band around her. He had his helpers stand on each side of Babe. He wanted to run under her with the rope that was tied to the big band. He thought he could get the rope and band under Babe before she knew what he was doing.

But Babe was too fast for Frank. When Frank walked under her, Babe reached down with her trunk and lifted him up high in the air. She seemed to say, "Now, how do you like being lifted in the air?"

Then, Babe threw Frank to the ground. She hurt him, but she did not kill him.

No one could get Babe on the ship, and so the ship left for the United States with Frank Buck and his animals. But Babe was still in Singapore.

Frank knew that Babe was not a bad elephant. He knew that she was just afraid of being lifted up into the air. He had to think of some other way to get Babe on a ship so he could get her to the park in San Francisco.

All the way to the United States, Frank Buck thought about Babe.

The next story will tell you how he got Babe to the United States.

Babe Gets to the United States

Babe was the elephant that did not like to be lifted up in the air. She was still on Frank Buck's farm in Singapore. Frank wanted to get her to a park in San Francisco.

Frank had left Singapore with his other animals, and, all the way to the United States, he thought about Babe. At last he thought of a way to get Babe on a ship for the United States. He wrote a letter to his friend in Singapore telling him just what to do.

And this is what happened.

A man went to the animal farm and made a platform of wood. Then, Babe was trained to stand on the platform. Every time Babe stood on the platform, she was given something good to eat, and so Babe liked to stand on the platform.

Then, one day while Babe was
standing on the platform eating, some
people made a strong wall of wood all
around the platform. Before Babe knew
what was happening, she was in a big
box.

The people made the box strong with iron bands so that Babe could not break out of the box. Then, the box was put on a big wagon and pulled down to the ship.

This time, the box with Babe in it was lifted up in the air and put on the ship. Babe squealed, but she could not break out of her big box.

Old Mon Comes to the United States

The manager of a circus wanted a new elephant. He wanted a very big elephant, and he wanted a smart elephant. So he sent a letter to a man in Germany who was very good at training animals.

The man in Germany sent a letter back to the manager and said that he had just the right elephant for him. It was a very big elephant. It was a very smart elephant, and it was a gentle elephant. It would do anything that the man wanted it to do.

Old Mamma, the elephant, was put on a big ship and came to the United States. The manager of the circus went to New York to help Old Mamma off the ship. He was very happy when he saw the elephant. He named her Old Mon.

She was the biggest elephant he had ever seen.

Then, things started to happen.

The big elephant would not move. The manager said, "Come. Let us go. Walk right. Walk left." But the elephant only looked at him. The manager shouted and waved, but Old Mon only looked at him.

The manager had to get the elephant off the ship. He had people put ropes around Old Mon. They lifted her off the ship and put her into a big wagon. Then they drove the wagon to the circus.

When the manager got to the circus, Old Mon would not get out of the wagon. All the animal trainers talked to Old Mon. Some of them talked, and some of them shouted. But the elephant would not move.

At last the people put ropes around the big elephant and pulled her out of the wagon. Then, they put ropes around her and pulled her where they wanted her to go. Old Mon did not fight. She was kind and gentle, but she just did not do what she was told to do.

One day, the manager of the circus read in the newspaper that the animal trainer from Germany was coming to New York. He wrote and asked the trainer to come where his circus was. He wanted to see the trainer and tell him about Old Mon.

When the trainer came, the manager took him to where Old Mon was tied.

"Why did you send me this elephant that will not do anything?" asked the manager of the circus. "I wanted an elephant that I could use in my circus. I wanted a smart elephant."

"What are you talking about?" asked the trainer. "This elephant is the best elephant that I have ever trained. She is smart, and she is gentle. We would even let her play with the children who came to see her. I never went by her without saying, '*Wie gehts, Mamma*' or '*Was ist los?*' and Old Mamma would put out her trunk to me."

Old Mon was standing right before the two men. She put up her ears. She was so happy that she squealed. She put her trunk around her old trainer. Then, Old Mon danced, lifting first one foot and then another foot. She was trying to thank the man who had said to her words that she knew.

"Then you always talked German to Old Mon?" asked the manager.

"Why, yes," said the trainer. "Old Mamma was caught in the forest by Germans. She was trained by Germans."

"Now I know what happened with Old Mon," said the manager. "She knows only German, and we have been talking to her in English."

"Elephants are smart," said the German trainer. "It is people who are not so smart. I did not tell you that Old Mamma was a German elephant when she came to you."

Both men laughed.

The manager of the circus got a trainer who knew German. He started to teach Old Mon English. First, he would tell Old Mon in German to do something. Then, he would say the same thing in English. Old Mon was a very smart elephant. It was not long before she knew English, and she always tried to do just as she was told. Old Mon was the smartest elephant in the circus.

Old Mon, the Queen of the Elephants

In every herd of elephants in the circus, there is one who is the queen. The bull-keepers of the elephants do not say who is queen. The elephants do.

It is the queen who walks at the head of the elephant herd. The queen looks after every elephant in the herd, and every elephant in the herd does what the queen says. If any elephant is bad, the queen will punish that elephant.

In Germany, Old Mon was the queen of the herd. When Old Mon got to the circus in the United States, Bumps was queen of the circus herd.

Old Mon did nothing but walk in the herd of elephants. The bull-keepers were afraid that with two queens there would be a fight, but Old Mon never did anything bad. She did just what Bumps wanted her to do.

Now, elephants do very hard things in the circus. They stand on their back legs. They stand on their front legs. They seem to dance to music.

It takes a long time to train animals. To teach an elephant to dance, a trainer stands in front of the elephant. The trainer holds a stick and moves the stick as if he or she were keeping time to the music of a band.

On each side of the elephant that is being trained is a person with an elephant hook. When the trainer's stick goes to the right, the person on the right side of the elephant lifts the elephant's right front leg with the elephant hook. When the stick goes to the left, the person on the left side of the elephant lifts the elephant's left front leg with a hook.

Elephants are smart, and it is not long before an elephant knows that when the stick goes to the right, it must lift its right leg. When you see an elephant dancing, the elephant is watching the stick in the trainer's hand, and the trainer is keeping time with the music of the band.

One elephant did not want to learn to dance. When the trainer went to get him, he cried. When the trainer took him back to the elephant herd, he cried and cried as if he had been hurt. Old Mon pulled up her iron stake where she was tied and went to see why this elephant was crying. She talked to him as elephants talk to one another, but he just cried and cried.

Then Old Mon went all over the elephant with her trunk to see whether the elephant hook had hurt him. She looked under his legs to see whether any ropes had hurt him. But Old Mon could not find that the elephant had been hurt. Old Mon knew that the elephant was just being bad.

So Old Mon hit the elephant with her trunk. She hit him so hard that he fell to the ground. Old Mon went back, put her stake in the ground and stood there as if nothing had happened.

The next day the circus was going to move down the road. The manager told the bull-keeper to have the elephants go first. There was a bridge on the road, and he wanted the elephants to cross the bridge first. If the elephants could cross the bridge, it would be all right for the big circus wagons to cross.

The bull-keeper got the herd of elephants ready. And who do you think was at the head? It was Old Mon. During the night, the other elephants had made Old Mon their queen. Bumps, who had been queen, walked behind Old Mon and did just what Old Mon told her to do.

Old Mon and the Bull-Keeper

The circus was in its winter home. The big circus wagons were being painted.

Old Mon and her bull-keeper were working hard. Mon was pushing the big wagons from one place to another. The bull-keeper was walking at her side to tell her what to do and which way to push the wagon.

Mon was very happy. She had some hay in her mouth and chewed it as she pushed a big wagon. The bull-keeper talked to Mon as they worked. He and Mon were great friends.

All of a sudden the circus wagon hit something and stopped. Mon gave a big push.

A big iron hook had been left on top of the circus wagon. When Mon gave the wagon a big push, the hook fell off the top of the wagon and hit the bull-keeper on the head. He fell to the ground and lay there.

Mon did not see the hook fall because her head was against the wagon, but she knew that something was not right. The bull-keeper was not telling her what to do. Mon stopped pushing the wagon and looked around. There on the ground was the man she loved.

Mon went to the bull-keeper. He did not move. Mon used her trunk to try to help him get up. Then, Mon raised her trunk and squealed and cried until people came running from all parts of the circus lot.

They saw the bull-keeper was on the ground and not moving. They saw Mon standing over him so no once could reach him to help him. Mon's trunk was raised high in the air and she was making a loud noise.

The people thought that Mon had killed her bull-keeper. They did not know what to do.

At last the bull-keeper opened his eyes. His head hurt and he could not see very well. There was a loud noise all around him. An elephant was crying, and people were shouting. At first he could not tell where he was and why a big elephant was standing over him.

Then, he remembered that Mon had been pushing the big circus wagon. It had suddenly stopped. That was the last thing he knew. Mon must be making all that noise.

The bull-keeper called to Mon. Mon
heard and stopped her noise. With her
trunk she helped the bull-keeper to his
feet. She went all over him with her
trunk to make sure he was all right. The
bull-keeper told Mon that his head
would be all right.

It was only then that Mon let the other people get near her bull-keeper. I can tell you that everyone was happy that the bull-keeper had not been killed.

White Elephants

This is a story about a white elephant that came to the United States.

There were two men who were always trying to outdo one another. Each man was manager of a circus. If one man got a big animal for his circus, the other man would try to get a bigger animal for his circus.

Now one of these men thought that he would get a white elephant for his circus. He knew that a white elephant would be the hardest thing in the world to get. He was sure that the other man could not get one.

This manager of the circus had people go to Thailand. They asked the king of Thailand to let them have a white elephant. They would give him a lot of money for it. The king said, "No."

But the circus people would not give up. They went to Myanmar, which is very near Thailand. The king of Myanmar wanted a lot of money. After much talking, he sold the people from the United States one of his white elephants.

The people did not know how to get the white elephant out of the country. They were sure that the people of Myanmar would not want a white elephant to go. So the people from the United States painted the elephant red and blue, and one night, they took the elephant down to a ship and left for the United States.

The manager of the circus put in all the newspapers that at last the people of the United States could see a white elephant, the king of elephants.

Now, when the other manager heard about this white elephant, he thought of something. He knew that he could not buy a white elephant, so he put white paint on an elephant to make it white. This was not smart, but it did not hurt the elephant.

You must know that a real white elephant is not white, but a very, very light gray. When the people of the United States went to see the real white elephant from Thailand, they saw a light gray elephant. But, when the people went to the other circus, they saw an elephant that was really white. They thought that a white elephant really was white.

What happened to the elephant that had been painted white? One day when the circus parade was going down the street, a sudden rain came. It washed the paint off the "white elephant." His skin under the paint was gray. People laughed and laughed. That circus manager never showed his white elephant again.

a
about
afraid
after
again
against
ago
air
Alice
Alice's
all
also
always
an
and
angry
animal
animals
another
any
anyone
anything
apple
are
around
as
asked
at
away
Babe
back
bad
band
bands
be
because
been

before
behind
being
beside
best
big
bigger
biggest
blue
both
box
break
bridge
Buck
Buck's
bull
Bumps
Burma
but
buy
by
called
came
can
cannot
cans
caught
chains
chewed
children
circus
circuses
city
come
comes
coming
could

country
cried
cross
crying
dance
danced
dancing
day
did
do
does
doing
done
down
drinking
drove
during
each
ears
eat
eating
elephant
elephants
elephant's
end
English
even
ever
every
everyone
everything
everywhere
eyes
fall
farm
fast
feet

fell
fight
find
first
five
flat
foot
for
forest
found
four
Frank
friend
friends
from
front
fun
gave
gehts
gentle
German
Germans
Germany
get
gets
getting
give
given
go
goes
going
good
got
gray
great
ground
had

hand	its
happen	jokes
happened	juice
happening	just
happy	keep
hard	keeper
hardest	keepers
have	keeping
hay	kept
he	kill
head	killed
hear	kind
heard	king
help	knew
helped	know
helpers	knows
her	last
herd	laughed
high	lay
him	learn
his	left
hit	leg
holds	legs
hole	let
home	letter
hook	lift
horses	lifted
how	lifting
hurt	lifts
I	light
if	like
in	liked
into	little
iron	live
is	lived
ist	log
it	logs

long

look

looked

looks

los

lot

loud

love

loved

made

make

making

Mamma

man

manager

many

mash

mashed

mashing

me

men

Mon

Mon's

money

more

most

mouth

move

moved

moves

moving

much

music

must

my

Myanmar

named

near

nearly

never

new

New York

newspaper

newspapers

next

night

no

noise

not

nothing

now

of

off

old

on

once

one

only

opened

or

other

out

outdo

over

owned

paint

painted

parade

park

part

parts

people

person

picked

place
platform
play
played
pull
pulled
punish
push
pushed
pushing
put
queen
queens
quietly
rain
raised
ran
Rangoon
reach
reached
read
ready
real
really
red
remember
remembered
riding
right
road
rope
ropes
run
running
said
same
San Francisco

saw
say
saying
says
see
seem
seemed
seen
send
sent
she
ship
shouted
shouting
showed
side
Singapore
skin
small
smart
smartest
so
sold
some
something
sometimes
squeal
squealed
squealing
stake
stand
standing
stands
started
starts
stick
still

stood
stopped
story
street
strong
stuck
such
sudden
suddenly
sure
take
taken
takes
talk
talked
talking
teach
tell
telling
tent
Thailand
thank
that
the
their
them
then
there
these
they
thing
things
think
this
thought
threw
thrown

tied
time
tired
to
told
too
took
top
train
trained
trainer
trainers
trainer's
training
tried
trunk
try
trying
two
under
United States
until
up
us
use
used
very
wagon
wagons
walk
walked
walking
walks
wall
want
wanted
warm

was
Was
washed
watching
waved
waving
way
we
well
went
were
what
when
where
whether
which
while
white
who
why

Wie
will
winter
with
without
wood
words
worked
working
world
would
wrote
Yangon
yellow
yes
you
zoo
zoos